YOUR PLACE in the UNIVERSE

JASON CHIN

NEAL PORTER BOOKS

HOLIDAY HOUSE / NEW YORK

For Vanessa Ford

I would like to thank Dr. Margaret Geller and Dr. Scott Kenyon
of the Harvard Center for Astrophysics for their time and expertise.
I could not have made this book without them.

Neal Porter Books

Text and illustrations copyright © 2020 by Jason Chin

All Rights Reserved

HOLIDAY HOUSE is registered in the U.S. Patent and Trademark Office.

Printed and bound in August 2023 at Leo Paper, Heshan, China.

The artwork for this book was created using watercolor, gouache, and digital techniques.

Book design by Jennifer Browne and Jason Chin

www.holidayhouse.com

First Edition

10

Library of Congress Cataloging-in-Publication Data

Names: Chin, Jason, 1978– author.

Title: Your place in the universe / Jason Chin.

Description: First edition. | New York City : Holiday House, [2020] |

Includes bibliographical references. | Audience: Ages 4–8 | Audience:

Grades K–1 | Summary: "A non-fiction introduction to the massive scale

of the known universe"— Provided by publisher.

Identifiers: LCCN 2019038030 | ISBN 9780823446230 (hardcover)

Subjects: LCSH: Cosmological distances—Juvenile literature. |

Astronomy—Juvenile literature. | Distances—Measurement—Juvenile

literature. | Universe—Juvenile literature.

Classification: LCC QB991.C66 .C45 2020 | DDC 530.8—dc23

LC record available at https://lccn.loc.gov/2019038030

ISBN: 978-0-8234-5245-3 (paperback)

These kids are eight years old.

They are about five times as tall as this book,

Eight-Year-Old
The average eight-year-old is about 50 inches (127 centimeters) tall.

but only half as tall as . . .

Inches

Inches are useful for measuring people and things that are smaller than people, like books.

. . . this ostrich. Ostriches are the tallest birds in the world, and may grow to be 9 feet tall.

That's taller than two eight-year-olds standing on each other's shoulders, but it's less than half as tall as . . .

This ostrich
is 100 inches (2.5 meters) tall.

. . . this giraffe.

Feet

One foot is equal to 12 inches. Feet are useful for measuring things
that are taller than humans, such as ostriches and giraffes.

Giraffes are the tallest animals on land. The tallest giraffe on record was 19 feet tall, which is more than twice as tall as the tallest ostrich, but giraffes aren't the tallest living things in the world.

This giraffe is 17.4 feet (5.3 meters) tall.

The tallest living things are trees.

The tallest trees on Earth are California redwoods, and the tallest redwood is 380 feet tall. It's 20 times taller than the tallest giraffe, and it's still growing, but even it is not as tall as . . .

This oak
is 100 feet (30.5 meters) tall.

This ceiba (kapok tree)
is 150 feet (45.7 meters) tall.

This giant sequoia
is 286 feet (87.2 meters) tall.

This Australian mountain ash
is 327 feet (99.8 meters) tall.

This redwood
is 380 feet (115.8 meters) tall.

. . . the tallest structures that humans have built.

The tallest building in the world is more than seven times taller than the tallest redwood, and people keep constructing taller buildings! But even these soaring skyscrapers are tiny compared to . . .

Eiffel Tower: 1,063 feet (324 meters)

Empire State Building: 1,454 feet (443.2 meters)

Burj Khalifa: 2,717 feet (828.1 meters)

Jeddah Tower (under construction): planned height 3,281 feet (1 kilometer)

. . . the highest peak on Earth.

Sea Level

Mount Everest: **29,035 feet (8,850 meters) above sea level**

Mount Everest is the highest peak on Earth measured from sea level. The tallest mountain measured from base to summit is Mauna Kea in Hawaii, but its base is below sea level. Its peak is 32,696 feet (9,966 meters) above the sea floor—3,661 feet taller than Mount Everest—but most of it is under water!

Measured from sea level, Mount Everest is 29,035 feet high. That's about 5.5 miles—almost nine times the height of the tallest planned building. But even Mount Everest doesn't reach all the way . . .

Miles

One mile is equal to 5,280 feet. Miles are useful for measuring longer lengths than feet, such as the distances between cities, the lengths of rivers, or the height of Mount Everest.

International Space Station

The ISS orbits in the thermosphere, 248 miles above Earth.

. . . to space.

Although there's no exact height for the edge of space, it's commonly said to be 62 miles up. The International Space Station orbits 248 miles above sea level. That's 45 times as high as Mount Everest, but it doesn't seem so far compared to . . .

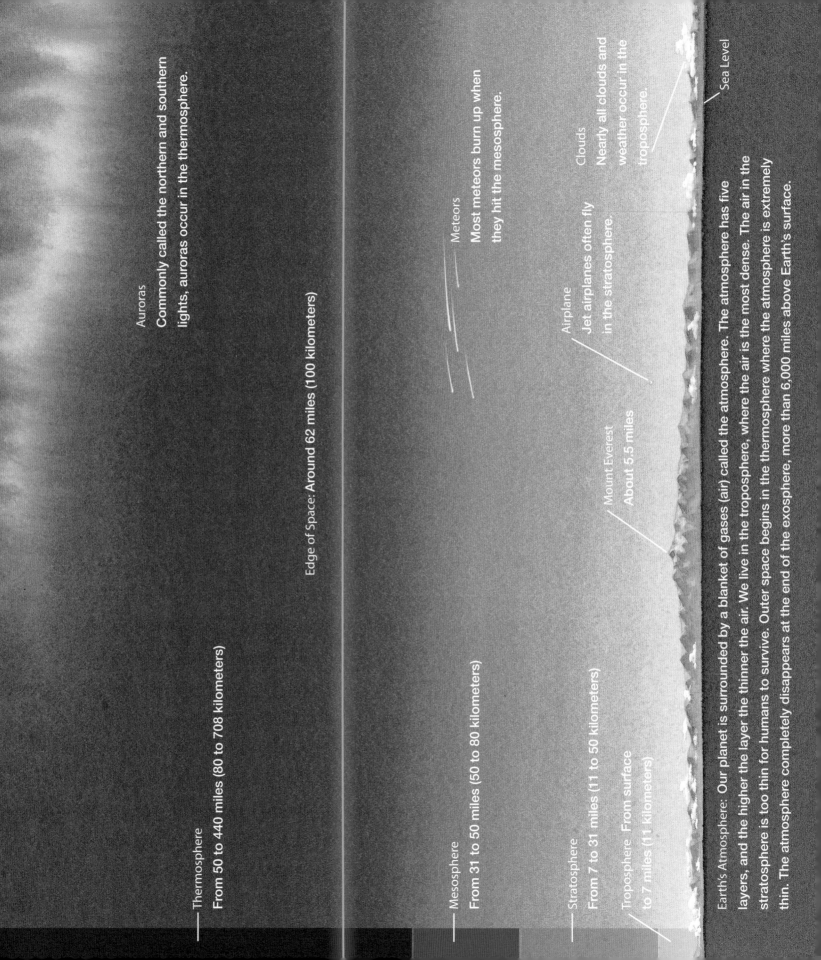

Thermosphere
From 50 to 440 miles (80 to 708 kilometers)

Auroras
Commonly called the northern and southern lights, auroras occur in the thermosphere.

Edge of Space: Around 62 miles (100 kilometers)

Meteors
Most meteors burn up when they hit the mesosphere.

Mesosphere
From 31 to 50 miles (50 to 80 kilometers)

Airplane
Jet airplanes often fly in the stratosphere.

Clouds
Nearly all clouds and weather occur in the troposphere.

Stratosphere
From 7 to 31 miles (11 to 50 kilometers)

Mount Everest
About 5.5 miles

Troposphere From surface to 7 miles (11 kilometers)

Sea Level

Earth's Atmosphere: Our planet is surrounded by a blanket of gases (air) called the atmosphere. The atmosphere has five layers, and the higher the layer the thinner the air. We live in the troposphere, where the air is the most dense. The air in the stratosphere is too thin for humans to survive. Outer space begins in the thermosphere where the atmosphere is extremely thin. The atmosphere completely disappears at the end of the exosphere, more than 6,000 miles above Earth's surface.

. . . the entire planet.

Earth is 7,926 miles wide. That's 128 times the distance from sea level to the edge of space. From far away, the visible atmosphere looks like a thin blue film surrounding our planet, and the International Space Station doesn't appear very far away at all. Earth is enormous, but it's not so big compared to . . .

Orbits
Satellites like the International Space Station travel around Earth in circular or oval paths called orbits. Gravity keeps satellites in orbit around our planet.

Hubble Space Telescope
353 miles (568 kilometers)
above sea level

International Space Station
248 miles (399 kilometers)
above sea level

Edge of Space
Around 62 miles (100 kilometers)
above sea level

Earth
7,926 miles (12,756 kilometers) across

Earth

A Natural Satellite

The Moon is a natural satellite of Earth, and it takes
27.3 days to make one trip around our planet. Gravity
keeps the Moon in orbit around Earth.

. . . the orbit of the Moon.

The Moon is 238,855 miles away from Earth. It's so far away that 29 Earths could fit between the two. It's so far that a jet plane going 500 miles per hour would take 19 days to get there. But even the Moon is close by compared to . . .

Moon
238,855 miles (384,400 kilometers) from Earth

Ceres
Average distance from the Sun:
257 million miles (414 million kilometers)

Mercury
Average distance from the Sun:
36 million miles (58 million kilometers)

Mars
Average distance from the Sun:
142 million miles (228 million kilometers)

Venus
Average distance from the Sun:
67 million miles (108 million kilometers)

Earth and Moon
Average distance from the Sun:
93 million miles (150 million kilometers)

Sun

The Inner Planets
The four closest planets to the Sun are Mercury, Venus, Earth, and
Mars. They are known as the terrestrial planets because they are
made of rock and metal, and have solid surfaces. Beyond the inner
planets are hundreds of thousands of rocky asteroids in the asteroid
belt. The largest object in the asteroid belt is the dwarf planet Ceres.

. . . the Sun.

Earth is 93 million miles away from the Sun. That's so far that a jet
plane going 500 miles per hour would take more than 20 *years* to get
there. It's so far that sunlight takes eight minutes to reach Earth,
and light travels 186,000 miles per second! But Earth is one of the
closest planets to the Sun.

Asteroid Belt

The Speed of Light
Light travels 186,000 miles per second. That's so fast that a beam of light
could circle Earth seven and half times in one second (if it could be made
to travel in a circle)! Nothing can travel faster than light.

There are five planets beyond Earth. The farthest is Neptune, which is 30 times farther from the Sun than Earth is. The dwarf planet Pluto is 40 times as far, which is so far that sunlight takes more than five and a half *hours* to reach it. Pluto is part of the Kuiper Belt, which has billions of comets and four dwarf planets, but that isn't the end of the solar system.

Eris
Average distance from the Sun: 6.3 billion miles (10.1 billion kilometers)

Earth, Sun, and Inner Planets

Pluto
Average distance from the Sun: 3.7 billion miles (5.9 billion kilometers)

Uranus
Average distance from the Sun: 1.8 billion miles (2.9 billion kilometers)

Saturn
Average distance from the Sun: 887 million miles (1.4 billion kilometers)

Neptune
Average distance from the Sun: 2.8 billion miles (4.5 billion kilometers)

Jupiter
Average distance from the Sun: 484 million miles (788 million kilometers)

The Outer Planets and Beyond
Jupiter, Saturn, Uranus, and Neptune are the farthest planets from the Sun. They are very big and very cold, and are surrounded by thick atmospheres. Beyond them are four dwarf planets—Eris, Pluto, Haumea, and Makemake—and billions of comets in the Kuiper Belt, and scientists believe that there are trillions of comets even farther away. These are the most distant objects in our solar system.

Scientists believe there are trillions of comets beyond the Kuiper Belt. The farthest of these could be 100,000 times farther from the Sun than Earth is. It takes sunlight more than a year to travel that far, which would make the edge of our solar system more than a light-year away. But our solar system is a tiny speck compared to the size of . . .

Haumea
Average distance from the Sun: 4 billion miles (6.4 billion kilometers)

Makemake
Average distance from the Sun: 4.3 billion miles (6.9 billion kilometers)

Kuiper Belt

The Light-Year
A light-year is a measure of distance (not time). It is the distance that light travels in one year—about 5.9 trillion miles. Astronomers measure the distances between stars and galaxies in light-years.

Sagittarius A*
The black hole at the center of the Milky Way

Our Solar System
27,000 light-years from the galactic center

The Milky Way Galaxy
Galaxies are groups of stars that are held together by gravity. The Milky Way is a
spiral galaxy, and just as the planets in our solar system orbit the Sun, the stars
in the Milky Way orbit the center of the galaxy. Hidden in the center of the Milky
Way is a black hole called Sagittarius A* (pronounced Sagittarius A-Star), which
is 4 million times more massive than the Sun.

. . . our galaxy.

The Milky Way galaxy is 100,000 light-years across and contains more than 100 billion stars. One of them is our Sun. There are so many stars that from a distance they blend together and look like swirling clouds of light. We are about 27,000 light-years from the center of the galaxy, which means that even if you could travel at the speed of light, it would take you 27,000 years to get there! But that's nothing compared with the distance to . . .

. . . the Andromeda galaxy.

Andromeda is the closest large galaxy to us, but it's 2.5 million light-years away—it would take you 2.5 million years traveling at the speed of light to reach Andromeda. Andromeda and the Milky Way are part of a galaxy group called the Local Group. It has roughly 50 galaxies, and is spread across millions of light-years of space, but galaxy groups are small compared to . . .

Andromeda
About 2.5 million light-years
from Earth

Milky Way

Looking Back in Time
Andromeda's light takes 2.5 million years to reach Earth. This means that when we look at Andromeda, we are seeing light that left it 2.5 million years ago, and the image that we see is 2.5 million years old—we're looking back in time!

. . . galaxy clusters.

Galaxy clusters are much larger than galaxy groups. The Virgo
Cluster is the largest galaxy cluster near us. It has around 2,000
galaxies and is roughly 50 million light-years away, but it's not
the only one. Many galaxy clusters and groups surround Virgo,
and all together they are known as the Local Supercluster.
But even our supercluster is just a tiny part of . . .

Local Group

Virgo Cluster
About 50 million light-years
from Earth

The Farther You Look . . .
The farther away you look, the farther into the past you'll see. If you look at
the Sun, you'll see it as it was eight minutes ago—you're looking eight minutes
back in time. If you look at Andromeda, you'll see 2.5 million years back in time.
If you look at Virgo, you're seeing 50 million years into the past.

. . . the cosmic web.

Huge chains of galaxies, millions of light-years long, are strung
throughout space. Clusters of galaxies are found where the chains
meet, and between the galaxies lie vast empty regions called voids.
This pattern is called the cosmic web, and it extends for billions
of light-years in all directions like a giant three-dimensional net.
These are the largest structures in . . .

Local Supercluster
We may be located in a void like this one.

The Cosmic Web
This illustration depicts the pattern of voids and chains of galaxies that make up the cosmic web, but not the actual position of galaxies. Evidence suggests that our supercluster is located within a large void, but we don't know for sure.

Edge of the Observable Universe
This is as far as we can see from Earth,
around 13 billion light-years away.

We are here.
But this is not the center of the
entire universe, just the center of
the part we can see.

The Observable Universe
The observable universe is the
part of the universe that we can
see from where we are. This region of
space is enormous, and it's estimated to
contain 2 trillion galaxies, but the universe
extends beyond what we can see. The
observable universe is centered on us, but we
are not in the center of the entire universe.

. . . the universe.

The universe is everything: every star and every galaxy, every planet, and all of space. It's the grandest environment we know of, and it may go on and on forever, but we don't know if it does. We don't know because the farthest we can see is around 13 billion light-years away. Everything within this distance is called the observable universe. It's the region of space that we can see . . .

. . . from where we are.

In the vast cosmic web, in the Milky Way, in the
solar system, there is a small blue planet called
Earth. Earth is the only planet that we know of
with life. It's the only planet we know of with
trees, giraffes, and ostriches. It's the only
planet we know of with kids who can look
up and imagine . . .

. . . their place in the universe.

BEYOND HUMAN SCALE

It's fairly easy to understand the size of things we interact with on a daily basis, such as books, buildings, and trees. These objects are on a human scale and it's not hard to measure them. Longer distances, like the height of Mount Everest or the distance to the edge of space, are far outside our everyday experience and are difficult to comprehend. Our solar system, our galaxy, and the universe are on a vastly larger scale and are even more difficult to imagine. By making accurate measurements, maps, and models, we can begin to understand size and distance at human scale and beyond. This helps us to understand not only our size, but also where we are. By measuring the distances to other planets, stars, and galaxies, astronomers have shown us the scale of the cosmos and begun to reveal our place in the universe.

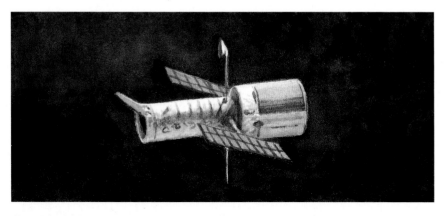

ASTRONOMY AND TELESCOPES

Astronomers are scientists who ask questions about what lies beyond Earth, including stars, planets, and galaxies. The telescope is the astronomer's most important tool. Stars and galaxies that are too small and too faint to see with our own eyes can be studied with the aid of a telescope. Telescopes have allowed astronomers to measure the distance to stars, planets, and galaxies and to learn where we are in the universe.

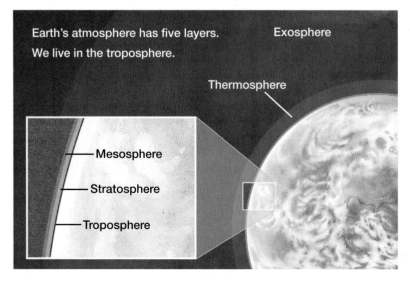

The Hubble Space Telescope is one of the most powerful telescopes ever built.

EARTH AND THE SOLAR SYSTEM

Earth is our home, and from our position on its surface, it's absolutely enormous. It is 7,926 miles (12,756 kilometers) across, and 24,900 miles (40,073 kilometers) around the equator. It would take 31 million eight-year-olds lying head to toe to circle the globe. The highest point on Earth is the peak of Mount Everest, and the lowest point is the bottom of the Mariana Trench in the Pacific Ocean.

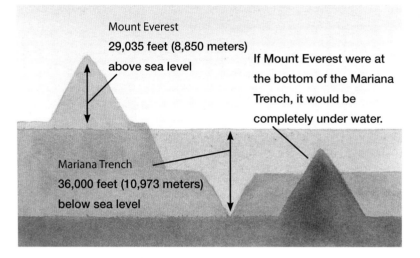

Mount Everest
29,035 feet (8,850 meters)
above sea level

If Mount Everest were at the bottom of the Mariana Trench, it would be completely under water.

Mariana Trench
36,000 feet (10,973 meters)
below sea level

EARTH'S ATMOSPHERE

Earth's atmosphere makes it possible for life to exist on our planet. Our atmosphere protects us from harmful solar radiation, it traps heat and keeps us warm, and it provides the air we need to breathe. Earth's atmosphere has five layers, and we live in the troposphere. Nearly all clouds and weather are in the troposphere, and it's the only layer where there is enough air for us to breathe, but the troposphere is just 7 miles high. If Earth were the size of a basketball, the troposphere would be about as thin as a postcard!

Earth's atmosphere has five layers.
We live in the troposphere.

Exosphere

Thermosphere

Mesosphere

Stratosphere

Troposphere

THE SOLAR SYSTEM

Our solar system is made up of the Sun and all of the objects that orbit it. There are eight planets, five known dwarf planets, more than a hundred moons, billions of comets, and hundreds of thousands of asteroids. The solar system out to the edge of the Kuiper Belt is like a flat disk, and this portion of the system is about 10 billion miles across. The Oort cloud is a spherical cloud of comets that scientists believe surrounds the Sun and its planets, and it's vast. Nobody knows where the Oort cloud ends, but estimates range from 930 billion to 9 trillion miles (about 1.5 light-years) from the Sun!

Earth

Inner Planets and Asteroid Belt

Outer Planets and Kuiper Belt

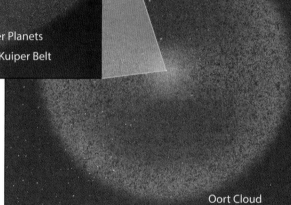

Oort Cloud

A GOLDILOCKS PLANET

Of all of the objects in our solar system, Earth is the one planet that is in the right spot to have liquid water—and that's why it can support life. If Earth were too close to the Sun, it would be so hot its water would evaporate away. If Earth were too far, it would be so cold its water would freeze. Earth is just right—it's not too close and not too far, not too hot and not too cold—which is why it's called a Goldilocks planet.

THE SUN AND PLANETS

The sizes of the planets vary tremendously. The dwarf planet Pluto is smaller than Earth's Moon, while the largest planet, Jupiter, is so big that more than a thousand Earths could fit inside of it. But the Sun is even bigger—more than a million Earths could fit inside of it!

Mercury · Venus · Earth · Moon · Mars · Jupiter · Saturn · Uranus · Neptune · Sun

Cosmic Web

Local Supercluster

Local Group

Milky Way

Solar System

THE UNIVERSE

The universe is all of space and everything in it. We can see only part of the entire universe, the part we call the observable universe. Space extends beyond what we can see, but since we can't see it, it's impossible to know where we are within the entire universe. Looking at an illustration of the observable universe, it may seem as if we are in the center of everything, but this is misleading. The observable universe is centered on us, but this does not mean we are in the center of the entire universe. In fact, astronomers don't think the universe has a center!

THE COSMIC WEB

Galaxies are arranged throughout space in a pattern called the cosmic web. Some regions of space, called voids, have relatively few galaxies, while other regions have dense collections of galaxies. We are in a group of galaxy clusters called the Local Supercluster.

GALAXY GROUPS AND CLUSTERS

Galaxy groups and galaxy clusters are collections of galaxies, and the gravity of all the galaxies pulling on one another holds them together. Galaxy groups have up to a few dozen galaxies; galaxy clusters have more. The Virgo Cluster has around two thousand galaxies, and our Local Group is near it.

GALAXIES

Galaxies are enormous collections of stars that are held together by gravity. They may have millions or billions of stars. Some have more than a trillion! Many galaxies, like our own Milky Way, have supermassive black holes at their center. Our Milky Way has more than 100 billion stars.

PLANETARY SYSTEMS

Planetary systems are stars with planets orbiting around them, like our solar system. Gravity holds the systems together. There are thousands of planetary systems beyond ours, and planets orbiting other stars are called exoplanets. So far, astronomers have discovered nearly four thousand exoplanets, and they expect to discover many more.

OUR COSMIC ADDRESS

In order for your friend to send you a postcard, she must know your address. She'll need to write down your house or building number, street, town, state, and possibly country. But what if an alien were writing from another galaxy? To get that letter to Earth, the alien would need to use our cosmic address, the address that tells our location in space.

Hello Earthlings!

Earth
The Solar System
The Milky Way
The Local Group
The Local Supercluster
The Universe

THE LIGHT-YEAR

A light-year is a measure of distance (not time). It's the distance that light travels in one year—about 5.9 trillion miles. Distances to stars and galaxies are often given in light-years. This tells us how far away they are and how long it takes for their light to reach us. For example, light from a star that is 10 light-years away takes 10 years to reach us.

LOOKING INTO THE PAST

Because light from stars and galaxies takes time to reach us, we always see them as they were in the past, not as they are today. For example, the Sun's light takes about 8 minutes to reach Earth. The light that we see now left the Sun 8 minutes ago, so the image of the Sun that we see is 8 minutes old—it's as if we are looking 8 minutes into the past. The farther away an object is, the longer its light has to travel and the farther into the past we see. The nearest star to the Sun (Proxima Centauri) is 4.2 light-years away, so we see it as it was 4.2 years ago. The Andromeda galaxy is 2.5 million light-years away, so we see it as it was 2.5 million years ago.

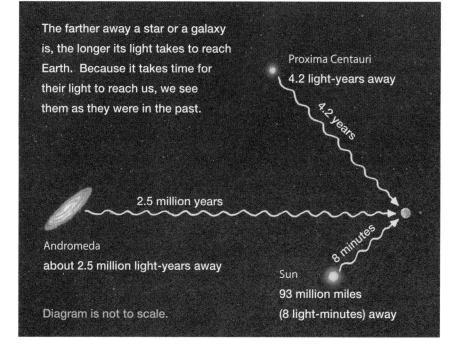

The farther away a star or a galaxy is, the longer its light takes to reach Earth. Because it takes time for their light to reach us, we see them as they were in the past.

Proxima Centauri
4.2 light-years away

4.2 years

2.5 million years

Andromeda
about 2.5 million light-years away

8 minutes

Sun
93 million miles
(8 light-minutes) away

Diagram is not to scale.

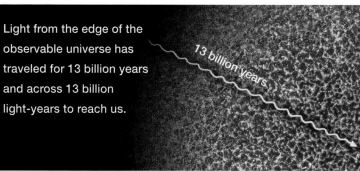

Light from the edge of the observable universe has traveled for 13 billion years and across 13 billion light-years to reach us.

13 billion years

THE FARTHEST WE CAN SEE

Astronomers believe the universe is around 13 billion years old (although there is debate about its exact age), and it's the age of the universe that limits what we can see. When we look farther and farther away, we see the universe as it was farther and farther back in time. Astronomers can look very far away, but if they tried to look beyond 13 billion light-years, they'd be looking to a time before 13 billion years ago. That's before the universe existed, so there is nothing to see beyond 13 billion light-years!

A NOTE FROM THE AUTHOR

Thinking about the size of the universe often makes me feel small. After all, there are billions of galaxies, each with billions of stars, many of which have planets orbiting them. We humans are just small animals, living on a small planet, with a thin blanket of air protecting us from the cold of space. I feel like an insignificant speck among all those stars and galaxies, until I remember how special it is that we are here and that we can imagine our place among all those stars. In all the universe, Earth is the only place that we know has life; and of all the living things we know of, humankind is the only species that understands the vastness of space. We can hold the cosmos in our minds, and we've begun to understand our place in it. That is very special, and although we are small, we are not at all insignificant.

A NOTE ON THE AGE OF THE UNIVERSE

The universe is commonly said to be 13.8 billion years old, but recent research suggests a younger universe (possibly as young as 12.5 billion years). For this book, I have chosen to use the round number of 13, but I expect that astronomers will arrive at a more precise number in the future.

A NOTE ON THE ILLUSTRATIONS

The illustrations in this book are intended to show the scale of objects and distances on Earth and in the universe, and each illustration is drawn to scale. I have, however, taken liberties in the depictions of the solar system and beyond to better convey the structure of the cosmos. The dots indicating planets, and the textures indicating the asteroid belt and Kuiper belt have been added. At this scale no planets, comets, or asteroids would be visible. The images of the Milky Way and beyond are artist interpretations, as direct observation of these scenes is impossible. My image of the Milky Way is based on photographs of galaxies with similar characteristics to ours. The images of our galactic neighborhood show only approximate locations of galaxies. The illustrations of the cosmic web and the observable universe show the pattern of galaxy distribution in space, but do not represent actual galaxies. They are based on computer models and renderings of redshift surveys such as the Sloan Digital Sky Survey.

SELECTED SOURCES

BOOKS

Bennett, Jeffrey, Megan Donahue, Nicholas Schneider, and Mark Voit. *The Cosmic Perspective: The Solar System*. 7th ed. New York: Pearson, 2014.

Bennett, Jeffrey, Megan Donahue, Nicholas Schneider, and Mark Voit. *The Cosmic Perspective: Stars, Galaxies and Cosmology*. 8th ed. New York: Pearson, 2017.

Chambers, John, and Jacqueline Mitton. *From Dust to Life: The Origin and Evolution of Our Solar System*. Princeton, NJ: Princeton University Press, 2014.

Gott, J. Richard. *The Cosmic Web: Mysterious Architecture of the Universe*. Princeton, NJ: Princeton University Press, 2016.

WEBSITES

Plants, Animals, and Buildings

- https://www.nationalgeographic.com/animals/
- https://plants.usda.gov/
- https://www.skyscrapercenter.com

Earth's Atmosphere

- https://www.nesdis.noaa.gov/content/peeling-back-layers-atmosphere
- https://scied.ucar.edu/atmosphere-layers
- https://www.weather.gov/jetstream/layers

Astronomy

- https://nssdc.gsfc.nasa.gov
- https://sci.esa.int/gaia/
- https://solarsystem.nasa.gov
- https://www.sdss.org/